Day of the Dead is celebrated in Mexico with a big street festival to remember the dead.

Martinmas is the feast of St. Martin, saint of the homeless. Children walk through the streets carrying lanterns.

Families in the United States of America celebrate Thanksgiving Day with a meal of turkey and pumpkin pie.

At the Chinese Moon Festival, children walk through the streets with lanterns and eat moon cakes.

Diwali is the Hindu festival of light. People make colour patterns outside their homes.

 Wherever you see this sign, it means you should ask for help from an adult.

Michaelmas dragon

Get ready

✔ Newspapers ✔ Paint and brush ✔ Scissors
✔ Cardboard tubes ✔ PVA glue and water (half in half)

...Get set

Make a donut ring from rolled newspaper.
Place it in the centre of a big sheet of newspaper,
tuck edges into ring and make a flat dish shape.
Repeat twice. Make a smaller 'dish' for a nose.
Glue on. Cover with papier mâché strips.
Do three layers. Leave it to dry. Cut eye holes.
Make cones of paper for ears and horns.
Cut cardboard tubes for nostrils.
Stick on with papier mâché strips.

 Go...

Add several more layers of papier mâché.
Paint with bright colours when dry.

4

Get set... Go!

Autumn Festivals

Helen Bliss

Photographs by Peter Millard

Contents

W
FRANKLIN WATTS

About Autumn festivals

Many of the Autumn festivals celebrate light. The activities in this book are inspired by the traditions of peoples round the world at Autumn.

Michaelmas is the feast of St. Michael. He is usually shown killing a dragon.

At Succot, Jewish people give thanks that the Israelites were sheltered in the desert. Little shelters are put up in the home or big ones built in the garden.

Hallowe'en was an ancient festival for the dead but is now a time when children dress up as witches and play tricks.

People have given thanks for a good harvest for thousands of years.

Succot hut

Get ready

✔ Bendy twigs   ✔ String   ✔ Fruit

✔ Glue   ✔ Leaves and flowers

...Get set

Weave the twigs together
to build the walls and roof
of the hut.
You may need to glue
or tie them together.

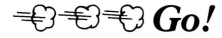 *Go!*

Decorate the hut with
flowers and leaves.
Place fruit around it.

Hallowe'en mobile

Get ready

✔ Black and shiny card   ✔ Sticky tape   ✔ Scissors

✔ Black thread   ✔ Pencil   ✔ Glue

...Get set

Cut a long strip of shiny card 1m x 7cm.

Cut a decorative edge.

Glue the ends together to form a ring.

Cut hallowe'en shapes from black card, such as cats and spiders.

Cut stars and moons from shiny card.

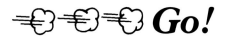 *Go!*

Hang the shapes on the ring using black thread and tape.

Tape thread to the top of the ring.

Hang your mobile up.

Magic hat

Get ready

- ✔ Scissors
- ✔ Pencil
- ✔ Stiff black paper
- ✔ 45cm length of string
- ✔ Glue
- ✔ Decorations

...Get set

Tie the string to the pencil.
Use it to draw a semi-circle and
a circle on the paper and cut both out.
Glue the semi-circle down the side
to make a cone the size of your head.
Draw round cone in the centre of the paper circle.
Draw another circle 2cm inside that one.
Cut round the inside line.
Cut flaps up to the outside line.

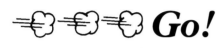 **Go!**

Use the flaps to glue the cone to the brim.
Decorate with glitter, sequins and sticky stars.

Harvest creatures

Get ready

✔ Vegetables and fruit, such as potatoes, corn, radishes, carrots and tangerines

✔ Cocktail sticks
✔ Nuts, raisins and parsley
✔ Knife

...Get set

Use a knife to cut some of the vegetables into arms, legs and feet for your creatures.
Use round vegetables as heads.
Join the pieces together with the cocktail sticks.

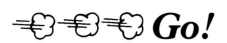 Go!

Add eyes and hair to your creatures using parsley, nuts and raisins.
Eat them afterwards!

Wiggle-waggle skeletons

Get ready

✔ Thin black card   ✔ Garden stick   ✔ Scissors

✔ Pencil   ✔ Hole punch   ✔ Sticky tape

✔ Paper fasteners   ✔ White paint   ✔ Paintbrush

...Get set

Draw your skeleton on to the card.
Copy this picture to help you.
Paint on a skeleton face and bones.
Punch holes, as in the picture.

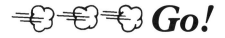 *Go!*

Tape the stick to the back of the body.
Push fasteners through the holes to connect
the body to the arms, legs and head.
Now wiggle-waggle!

Martinmas lanterns

Get ready

✔ Coloured card   ✔ Sticky tape   ✔ Pencil

✔ Tissue paper   ✔ Ruler   ✔ Scissors

✔ Glue stick   ✔ Garden cane

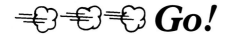

...Get set

Cut a rectangle of card.

Draw flower, moon and animal shapes on to it.

Cut them out and glue tissue paper behind them.

Join the ends of the card together
with glue to form a tube.

⇒🌀⇒🌀⇒🌀 *Go!*

Cut a handle and glue inside the top.

Tape the stick to the handle.

Turkey collage

Get ready

✔ Large sheet of orange paper   ✔ Pencil and felt-tips

✔ Coloured tissue paper   ✔ Glue and gluebrush

✔ Paint and brush

...Get set

Draw a turkey shape on to the paper.
Paint the neck, head and feet.
Leave it to dry.
Scrumple up the tissue paper
into little balls.

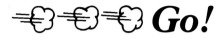 Go!

Build up your collage by sticking the little
balls on to your turkey.
Draw on his eye with felt-tip.

Moon Festival lanterns

Get ready

✔ Pen torch   ✔ Blown up balloon   ✔ Scissors

✔ Masking tape   ✔ Garden cane   ✔ Tissue paper

✔ PVA glue and water (thick mixture)

...Get set

Cover the balloon with small papier mâché strips of tissue paper, making 5 layers in total.
Leave to dry and cut a hole, as shown above.
Decorate with tissue paper scales and feathers.

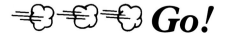 *Go!*

Tape the torch to the stick.
Push them into the lantern.
Make a small hole where the stick touches the top of the lantern.
Push it through and secure with tape.

Diwali flour patterns

Get ready

- ✔ White flour
- ✔ Red, yellow, blue and green powder paint
- ✔ 4 dry bowls
- ✔ Tablespoon
- ✔ Pencil
- ✔ Scissors
- ✔ Large sheet of paper
- ✔ Sieve

...Get set

In a bowl, mix 4 tablespoons of red powder paint with 8 tablespoons of flour.
Repeat with the other colours in separate bowls.
Draw a large flower on your paper.
Cut it out to form a stencil.

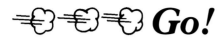 **Go!**

Place the stencil on a flat surface outside.
Shake the red flour through the sieve over part of the stencil.
Build up a pattern with the other colours.

Index

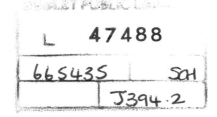
This edition 2003
Franklin Watts
96 Leonard Street
London EC2A 4XD

Franklin Watts Australia
45-51 Huntley Street
Alexandria
NSW 2015

©1993 Watts Books

Editor: Pippa Pollard
Design: Ruth Levy
Cover design: Mike Davis
Artwork: Ruth Levy

ISBN 0 7496 5281 0

A CIP catalogue record for this
book is available from the
British Library

Printed in Malaysia

Acknowledgements :

The author and publisher
would like to thank the pupils
of Kenmont Primary School,
London and Camilla, Marcus
and Mimi for their participation
in the photography of this
book.

24